Palewell Press

The Ghost of Franz Kafka
New Poems

Patric Cunnane

The Ghost of Franz Kafka – New Poems

Published by Palewell Press Ltd
http://www.palewellpress.co.uk/

First Edition

ISBN 978-1-911587-00-2

All Rights Reserved. Copyright ©2018 Patric Cunnane. No part of this publication may be reproduced or transmitted in any form or by any means, without permission in writing from the author.

The right of Patric Cunnane to be identified as the author of this work has been asserted by him in accordance with the Copyright, Designs and Patents Act 1988

Cover design Copyright © Camilla Reeve 2018
Front cover picture: Poulnabrone Dolmen, the Burren, Co Clare, Ireland. Photograph: Patric Cunnane
Back cover picture: Author in Peckish vegan restaurant, Ennis, Co Clare, Ireland. Photograph: Ruth Clydesdale.

A CIP catalogue record for this title is available from the British Library.

Palewell Press Ltd supports the Forest Stewardship Council® (FSC®) the leading international forest-certification organisation. Our books carrying the FSC® label are printed on FSC®-certified paper. Their printing and binding complies with ISO 14001 (Environmental Management) and 50001 (Energy Management).

Dedication

This book is dedicated to Ruth, to the memory of Nora and Martin, to my friends and family and to Bob, my (hardly ever) faithful border collie.

Acknowledgements

'When You Hang a Poet' was included in the collection *Dance Music* by Patric Cunnane, published by Dodo Modern Poets, 1999. 'Time and the Man' was previously published in the anthology, *Climbing the Sky in Colours*, Fal Publications, 2014. 'Longing for Cuba' and 'Come Home, John Keats' appeared in the anthology, *Poets in the Afternoon*, Red Corpuscle press, 2014. 'First Cup' appeared in *Gull* zine, 2016. 'Ulysses in Folkestone' appeared in *Out Of Luck* magazine, July 2017.

Contents

PART I - BETWEEN SANITY AND MADNESS 1
Keys 2
Smoking Gun 3
Refugee 4
No More Superheroes 6
Mineworker 7
When You Hang a Poet 8
Light Your Fires 10
The Darkest Stars 12
PART II - THE WORLD ALIGHT 13
My Father's Mansions 14
Time and the Man 15
Our Neighbour Bill 16
Lament for Seamus 18
Donaghy 19
Come Home, John Keats 20
Unthinking Light 21
National Poetry Day 22
PART III - THE OLD COUNTRY 23
A March Night in Dublin 24
First Cup 25
Birthday Fuck 26
Old Men in Café 27
Vikings in Ireland 28

Windmills	30
Picking Mushrooms in Tubbercurry	31
Absence of Joe	32
PART IV - PINKING IN SUNLIGHT	33
Kalloni	34
Watermelon	35
Turkish Breakfast	36
Melon	37
Birthday in Mytilene	38
Bacon on the Orient Express	39
Longing for Cuba	40
The Falling	42
PART V - THOSE THAT REMAIN	43
First Date	44
Supermarket Love	45
Old Anthology in Oxfam Bookshop	46
The Old Office	47
Holding Hands with Barbara	48
Foot	49
Michelangelo	50
Ulysses in Folkestone	51
The Ghost of Franz Kafka	52
More in Sorrow	54
PART VI - WHERE I AM	55
A Moment With My Map	56
Tigers	57

The Fools	58
The Kids Are Alright	59
Regrets	60
Yeah Yeah Yeah	61
Someone, Somewhere in Gold Trainers	62
Messages from Paradise	63
Sawing Wood	64
REFERENCE	65
Patric Cunnane - Biography	66

New Poems

PART I - BETWEEN SANITY AND MADNESS

The Ghost of Franz Kafka

Keys

I closed the front door
Never knowing if I'd walk through again

I took a rucksack, phone, house keys
The one part of home that's portable

I hang them in my new room
Under a picture of the city we fled

I turn them in an imaginary lock
Picture the door swinging open
My wife smiling, my children playing
Voices trickling in from the garden

Life goes on, we are safe for now
When someone shouts, 'Go home, go home'
I pretend I can't understand

At least their words aren't bombs
Their insults backed up by guns

Inspired by 'Just 1 Thing', a refugee exhibition in St Mary's Church, Dover. Refugees often take their house keys when leaving their homes.

New Poems

Smoking Gun

They say smoking is bad for you
But imagine you're in a refugee camp
And someone hands you a cigarette

What do you do?

You smoke the fucker, greedily, eagerly
Because that's all you have
Between sanity and madness

You smoke the fucker
Calmly, after the first desperate drag
Appreciate the friendly fire, tickling your lungs

You think, well it's not as bad as phosphorous gas
Or losing your sons

What do you do if someone hands you a gun?
And you're in a refugee camp, forever
You and five million others

You imagine you might pull the trigger
And you're no longer in that refugee camp
You're in that place even rich people can't escape

Out of 22.5 million refugees worldwide, 5.3 million are from Palestine, by far the largest group. Sources: UNHCR (UN Refugee Agency) and UNRWA (United Nations Relief and Works Agency for Palestinian Refugees in the Near East)

Refugee

Refugee is
Living in fear every second of every day

Refugee is
Seeing your children killed
Terrified for the ones that live

Refugee is
Realising Escape is a place with no name

Refugee is
Fleeing with just a suitcase and your loved ones

Refugee is
Losing all you own, your home, its memories

Refugee is
Giving your money to a gangster
Letting that gangster risk your life in a leaky boat

Refugee is
The jubilation of survival as you scrabble onto dry land

Refugee is
The kindness of islanders offering shelter & warmth

Refugee is
Continuing your journey on a pitiless road

Refugee is
Bullet-faced men guarding razor-wire fences

New Poems

Refugee is
Watching a continent pull up its drawbridge

Refugee is
Freezing camps in winter, all dignity stripped away

Refugee is
Wicked politicians peddling a currency of hate

Refugee is
The miracle of completing the obstacle course

Refugee is
Being lifted by strong hands, words soothing as balm
Welcome friend, welcome home, come share our land

No More Superheroes

Finally, you accept there are no superheroes
No one to swoop beneath the 'plane
Single-handedly guide it to land
No one to right the capsized boat
Rescue the passengers, set it afloat

No one to quench the fire
Unswirl the sandstorm, splice the floes
Push water up the mountain

Your eyes have fully opened
Trust only takes you so far
Faith and credibility are orphaned
The once mighty shorn of their locks

And no one, nowhere, can mend a broken heart

Mineworker

Her beauty shines among the smoked-out terraces
Clear eyes, scraped hair, scarf tied above her ears
Kiss curl softening brow, eyebrows arched with dust

She works in darkness but lives in light
A profile suggesting the woman that might be

No privilege, just the hope of never starving
Of not being under a collapsing roof, a falling beam

The artist grants her
The dignity and strength of one
Who sees some higher purpose for her class

When labour will have value
Fly its flag from a steadier mast

Till then this girl stays rooted to her landscape
Shouting across valleys to the seats of power
Fiery reds and muddy blues denoting
Something yielding, not locked in time

Inspired by Belgian painter Constantin Meunier's 'Mineworker'

When You Hang a Poet

When you hang a poet
You have not shut his mouth

When you strip his dancing body
From the gallows
You have not shut his mouth

When your thieves of the light
Set his laughing corpse on fire
You have not shut his mouth

When, weighted with your guilt,
You sink his singing ashes
To the ocean floor
You have not shut his mouth

You have opened a door
You have awoken every poet
Who will in turn awake a thousand more

Shelley's 'unacknowledged legislators
Of the world' for Africa's sake
Demand that this be heard:

New Poems

When you hang a poet
You have not shut his mouth
Listen, he is speaking to you now!
You have opened a door through which
One day, freedom will walk

For Benjamin Moloise, hanged 18 October 1985 in South Africa. Written on a bus to Croydon the same morning after hearing Benjamin's mother on the radio, following her son's death. She said the tragedy would inspire the struggle to go on.

Light Your Fires

Impatient with her jurors, Joan snapped, "Light your fires."
So they did. Burned this roaring girl, not yet twenty

She was fitted up
The court translated her middle-French into Latin
Not a tongue she understood

Bored by repeated questions she languidly replied
"Ask me next Saturday."

Pressed about the voices, what form they took
If they had names, entered through doors,
Were warm or aromatic, she said
"The light comes in the name of the voice."

And what language did the voices speak?
"Better language than yours."

She was judged a heretic, scorched in the square
"Light your fires," she scorned, ascending into sainthood

Once she convinced the Dauphin
She was sent by God to quell the English

In body armour and shorn hair, just seventeen
She faced them off at Orleans
A court would later confuse, amuse and kill her
But that day her voice could not be clearer:

"The King of Heaven commands you, through me
To abandon your strongholds, go back to your country.
If not, I'll make a war cry, remembered forever."

France's anointed heroine won the day
Her only sin? She embarrassed men
She wrote the script, she made the play

The Darkest Stars

Through these flames we seek freedom
Our immolated flesh singeing darkest stars

Our voice is speaking, listeners recoil
At this challenge to our rude imprisonment
The scorching of our precious soil
Our exiled leader's eloquent resistance

As a new year turns, spare a prayer for us
Set it spinning on your wheel
Understand our desperate plea
Our reddening anger, our white-hot steel

Since 2011 at least 150 Tibetans have self-immolated in Tibet and China, many of them young monks or nuns. Most died from their injuries. Source: www.savetibet.org

New Poems

PART II - THE WORLD ALIGHT

The Ghost of Franz Kafka

My Father's Mansions

An electrician working sites
My father connected the future
To the miracle of light

Gone before we rose for school
Beloved leader until illness stole him away
And I shivered in a brown suit at his funeral

What were his days like?
Did he join his mates at a café?
What did they talk about?

The old country, I suppose
For there were lots of Irish in that job
When they finished building this country
You'd find them down the pub

My father's shades are everywhere
Lean-faced men, grubby from work
Useful men who can wire a house

I imagine my father's day
The manly reality of him
Building structures that survive

My father's mansions held many rooms
He lit them all

Time and the Man

My mother bought broken clocks at jumble sales
My father mended them
Spent hours fiddling with the mechanisms
Uncoiling the stuck springs

With his sharp electrician's eye
And nimble fingers, used to separating wires
He pried apart the innards until discovering
The secret hurt at the heart of time

Hours later, at teatime
We tiptoed in, found him trance-like
Hand cupped to the mechanism
Released from its cage of inactivity
Tick-tocking rhythmically, majestically

Setting time going as shadows crossed the room
And we longed for our Saturday sausages
And the coming of the moon

Our Neighbour Bill

Here, where we are tonight,
William Morris set the world alight
Producing textiles for discerning homes
Some whose furniture included thrones

The Queen hung his paper in Balmoral
Rankling with the great man's morals
All the time his socialist heart
Insisted workers should share his art

He believed that wealth caused sin
And set to write the story out
How capital would take a rout

In *News from Nowhere, Dream of John Ball*
He showed how power would take a fall

By the Wandle he created jobs
For human beings, not cogs
Kelmscott Manor, the Red House
Designed to show
Beauty and utility together go

Marxist realist, friend of Engels
Medieval dreamer, political schemer,
Skillful weaver of art and verse
Our neighbour Bill was all these things

Sharing life with passionate friends
Rosetti, Janey and Burne Jones
So much talent in these few homes

How many lives did William lead?

Enough to write two epic poems
The Earthly Paradise, The Golden Loom
And splendid versions of Nordic tales
Set dancing to a mighty tune

He formed the Art Workers' Guild, the Socialist League
Permitting art to live, ideas to breathe

Rich was the work but time was thin
No man of flesh fits so much in

Dead at 58. A physician said
He died of being William Morris I think
Not pleurisy, gout or too much drink
There goes a man who never stopped
Till time's winged chariot called a halt

On Wandle's banks he laid his schemes
Tonight, we honour William's dreams
The river rolling through his life
Belongs to you, as he hoped and knew
That liberty should make us proud
Let's say it here, let's say it loud

And raise a glass to William Morris
A roaring lion with a poet's kiss

This poem was written for a show at Merton Abbey Mills, London, close to where William Morris began production in the 19th century.

Lament for Seamus

In memory of Seamus Heaney 1939-2013

As summer passed, so did you
Leaving, as you always did
A generous space for others

Once, I saw you read in London
A benign god descended from the mountain
Coupling links of the human chain

Your work travelled well
In Florence, we sat up late
Drinking wine, entranced
By your voice and Liam's piping

Poems that lingered in the night
Causing me to rise at dawn
Pen my own verse, giddy
With the richness of language found

And now, sad day, I come home
Weighed down with groceries
Hear your name on the news
Which cannot be good news

What's a poet doing amid the lunchtime wars and warring?

You are gone and now forever here
Leaving us alone with summer's beauty
The certain truth you fashioned from your poetry

New Poems

Donaghy

In memory of Irish American poet, Michael Donaghy

I read first, Donaghy followed
Recited beautiful verse
Struck up tunes on his fiddle

Dark hair speaking to his roots
A green Yankee in London

Afterwards, Guinness flowed
Donaghy full of charm, one of us
The table awash with comfortable words

We hoped to meet again, poet to poet, becoming friends

Now Donaghy's gone, taken too soon
The link between tradition and Ireland's young

I peruse his collected, elegantly bound
But would rather Donaghy here
Opening his fiddle case, moistening the bow
Lifting a pint, in no hurry to go

Come Home, John Keats

In Keats' bedroom
Standing by his pale death mask
Looking over the garden
Counting steps in the snow

I'm tempted to bounce on the bed
Wake up, John Keats!
Don't huddle by the fireplace
With its pale sand mantelpiece
Pine cones heaped in the grate

Ignore the salon below
Where you reclined when sick
Knock off another *Endymion*
4,000 lines can't hurt you now

Don't linger in Rome
They have plenty of poets of their own
We'll club together for a flight
Have you back in no time

Come home, John Keats
The best bottle in the cellar purrs a welcome
What do you *mean*, your name is writ in water?
Your name is writ in beauty, a joy forever

Keats is buried in Rome. His tombstone reads: 'Here lies One Whose Name was writ in Water' There is no name. (Author's note: the capitals on the inscription are as on the tombstone)

Unthinking Light

This light strikes me as being wary
In what it chooses to reveal

Ships and cities
Drift in and out
Of its gaze

It doesn't care who knows
That it doesn't care

National Poetry Day

Taking a cab from the station
I tell the driver I've been at poetry readings all day
"What is poetry?" he says.

Now I'm on the spot, what *is* poetry?
Emboldened by drink, I say,
"Poetry is music but words without music."
He thinks for a moment:
"You like music then?"

"Yes, but that's not it, not poetry exactly."
He changes gear, we listen to Muzac FM

Poetry is a moment when someone says
Something so extraordinary, you write it down
I don't say this out loud
"That'll be five quid," he says, pulling into the kerb.

"Thanks," I say, "*This* is what poetry is all about."
I say this out loud and he recognises a drunk
If ever he's ever seen one.

New Poems

PART III - THE OLD COUNTRY

The Ghost of Franz Kafka

A March Night in Dublin

A tin can ricocheting down the road
The sussuration of blowyness

Girls' voices rising from the street
Seeking the party that is Tuesday

Red wine trickles on red sheets
As we huddle in this cold room

Feel the mighty thrum-swash of the Liffey
Wrestling with her sea-borne demons

Where's the craic? Here in a room
Where the window doesn't open

The one radiator beaten into submission

That tin can again, endless ricocheting
The girls' voices, laughing now

You listen for the noises you can't hear
Noises saying, this is this city, no other

A bottle drops, ker-krashing
Before the tin can chimes in

A note of music hangs for two beats
A gull sets up an answering cry

The city has chosen a palette answering only to itself
And does a dog bark somewhere in the Wicklow hills?

First Cup

Blue light comes on
Morning kettle
Clearing its throat

Filigree silkiness
Of tea bag
Dropping into cup

Peaty mug of Irish
Tasting of fresh boiled earth

Birthday Fuck

We've made an igloo of our love
Within it we fuck deliciously
Snowed under with icy thrills

March, Dublin

Old Men in Café

Every afternoon ruminating
On their version of the world

They make one drink last
Customers come and go
They remain, implacable as Rushmore

Curling slow tongues round words
As hours lean toward evening

Chewing the cud of existence
Present informed by the past

Wild times seen through a haze
Unlikely to rattle cages
Unless the coffee runs out

Vikings in Ireland

Despite founding its capital
The Vikings were denied a thousand welcomes
The Irish being no fans of slave trading or unsalted butter

They were fond of the dark stuff
Which they'd one day brew and market all over the world
They had no need of Scandinavian verse
Having many blood-curdling epics of their own
And long memories which didn't forget a single syllable

The Vikings had to make do with taking what they could
While suffering the odd bloody nose
They had to learn to chase armies into the hills
Only to see them disappear into the bogs and mist
To the sound of echoing red-haired laughter

Such were the perils of invasion
Of settling in the dark pool

Denied a thousand welcomes
At all times under a cloud
No one impressed by their sexy longboats
How fast they sailed up river and out to sea

Not a thing the Vikings could do to get themselves liked
Women spat on their shoes, men went on digging peat

A thousand welcomes? You must be joking

Cool disdain and muttered imprecations
Were the best they could expect
As they sat on the Liffey and scratched their heads
Watching the sun set neutrally over Wicklow mountains
Making no distinction between visitors and visitees.

Windmills

Here there are windmills
Tilting at the sun

And a lone cyclist
Eating up the miles to home

Letting the canal
Drift by without thought

New Poems

Picking Mushrooms in Tubbercurry

We fetched a bucket to the field
Rain sparkling in hedgerows
Began picking dew-fresh gold
Luscious funghi, free as the western air
Teasing my grandmother's house

Atlantic girlishly tossing her whitecaps
As we returned, ripe with treasure

Stoked the fire with peat
Placed a brimming pan on the hob
Mushrooms wallowing in a scoop of dripping

Breakfast served with soda bread
Butter melting into pale streams
My uncle ate from the frying pan
Smoked for a while

Then took his keen-edged spade down to the turf

A life lived without telephone or television
Radio or papers, only gossip for news

Content in its natural rhythms, ceilidh, church going, hymns

Tubbercurry is in Co Sligo, Ireland

Absence of Joe

Half seven there's an absence of Joe
We're not worried, he's not expected yet

At the appointed time
In walks someone who's not Joe
Followed by a man who should be Joe but isn't

We wait while several not-Joes enter
Are greeted by other not Joes

I leave a message on Joe's phone
Where are you? We're puzzled by your absence

Joe rings, he's missed a connection
Promises to ring back in the morning

Next day the clock ticks towards noon
No word from Joe

His absence lingers, is eventually washed away
By relentless Irish rain

Having missed our connection with Joe
We return to England with only
A litre of Powers' whiskey for company

New Poems

PART IV - PINKING IN SUNLIGHT

Kalloni

The backgammon players are attended to
By the kind waitress
Her smile sweetening their coffee

Her slim frame slipping between wreaths
Of cigarette smoke

The old timers chew their stubs toothlessly
She has a grace word for each

Time hangs heavy through the siesta
Counters and dice clicking to an antique rhythm

A pack of dogs gathers to piss on one motorbike

Click and throw, click and throw
The serious business of gambling on this slow afternoon

Feeling like the moment before the baddies ride in
And the sheriff steps out to meet them

September, Kalloni, Lesvos

Watermelon

On a winter's night, your table is blessed
With tropical greens and reds
You think of all the things you could say
About a watermelon, the poems you could write
About this gorgeous fruit

How it travels like a cold drink in your heart
Injects rhythms of smiles into breathing stars

The beauty of the watermelon
Cannot be expressed in verse
It seeds its magic from another galaxy
One in which red is the dominant colour
And the sun is made of a million juice petals

Turkish Breakfast

Morning is a bit of a Turkish breakfast
Cloudy, rain on the wind, shape shifting
Your panties lie on the floor, your bra on a chair

I make tea, watch the miracle of you sleeping

December, Mytilene, Lesvos

Melon

Maria leaves a melon in our room
A present from her garden

It sits by the window, softly yellow
In afternoon light

Over many breakfasts
We honour its flesh with yoghurt
Till all is gone

Leaving a melon-shaped hole in our fridge

O, proud melon of Lesvos
We salute you!

August, Lesvos

Birthday in Mytilene

On your birthday
We drank tea in the harbour café

Watched fishing boats glide to sea

The church's onion dome pinking in sunlight

A bird flying carelessly across the sky

Into our tea
We dunked biscuits shaped like teaspoons

December, Mytilene, Lesvos

New Poems

Bacon on the Orient Express

Bacon on the Orient Express
Gazing into the lens
Of a black and white world

We can't see his companion
But Frank looks pretty happy
Four wine bottles share the foreground

Nineteen sixty-five
The painter very much alive
Decades to go before expiring in Madrid
Frankie on a day out, happy as a kid

Inspired by a photograph in the exhibition 'Changing States – Contemporary Irish Art & Bacon's Studio', Bozar, Brussels

Longing for Cuba

'My whole being is filled with want of Cuba' -
Ana Mendieta, 20 March 1981

Home after twenty years
The artist fills her heart and art
With natural materials
Carves sculptures into limestone caves
In Jaruco National Park

Reactivates Taino goddesses
Rescues the black Siboney venus
From an abandoned colonial grave

How the heart longs for homeland
Misses the nurture of childhood years
Spirited to America at thirteen
From the flame of revolutionary Cuba
Into the maw of its bullying neighbour

The artist writes in a poem:
'My whole being is filled with want of Cuba.'

Who can blame her?

The teenage hurt of being wrenched from home
For the sake of nameless fears

She seizes the moment
Returns again and again
Loves the crocodile-shaped island
Bonds with its artists
Reclaims her birthright

She writes in that same poem:
'The art of thinking is to see ideas
Grow from root to fruit.'

The island embraces her energy
She offers it the fire of her youth.

The Falling

and I long and yearn - Sappho, fragment 16

The cleansing rain
Falls and falls and falls
A rush of joyous noise

The street is a river
Into which we step gingerly
Clutching wine & candles & water

How I have longed for such simplicity
Everything torn away, fallen
The apple uneaten

December, Mytilene, Lesvos

新 Poems

PART V - THOSE THAT REMAIN

First Date

At first, I didn't know you from Adam
An easy mistake, not having met Adam

Turns out you're Eve and I'm Adam
Original designs found in this garden

The nights are pretty quiet
Maybe we could order pizza or fruit
Do you like apples?

Let's share some juicy times. What do you say,
Your lawn or mine?

Supermarket Love

Travelling in matching fleeces
Shop workers romancing on the bus

Shoulder to shoulder, her red hair
Tumbling down his back

He smiles into her eyes
Pupils shining like new planets

Monday's shift can't dent their happiness
Tarnish their first taste of love

One day they will separate, go their ways

This is enough for now, young lives
Banking promises of future summers

Old Anthology in Oxfam Bookshop

Where now, the recently famous?
Their once-starry names collected here
Achievements detailed at the rear
A new selected out next year

Whither the golden evenings
Beset by acolytes at readings
Matily slugging beer
Exploring hidden meanings

How travel from there to here?
Ignored by Generation Now
Who scoop the plaudits
While their ancestors slumber
On shelves where nothing's new

Those that remain upside of grass
Realise verse is rarely meant to last
They once were ones to watch
Now they're guardians of the past

The Old Office

It felt solid, the old office
Workers bashing typewriters
Where personnel now surf the net

Spam curdling in the bin
Blinds to keep the greyness in

You could count on its blockiness
Lockable cabinets, no valuables inside
The stationery cupboard
An Aladdin's cave for secret poets

Lunchtime routines
Swilling it back in the pub
Plates of greasy grub
None of your prat in a manger

So many changes

We used to go in Saturday mornings
Wages arrived in brown envelopes
Cash was king
Best not spend it all on a weekend fling

Oh, it was solid all right
Workers bashing typewriters
Where personnel now surf the net

Ladies' perfume losing out
To boozy fumes and reek of fags
It was a ripe enough time for us old lags

The Ghost of Franz Kafka

Holding Hands with Barbara

I lay my palm over the artist's bronze hand

Do I imagine a tremor
A twitch, an impulse to return to work?

The hand is a cast of the artist's own hand displayed at the Barbara Hepworth Museum, St Ives, Cornwall. The museum was formerly Hepworth's studio and home.

Foot

I offer this plaster to the gods
In thanks for the foot, once crushed
By a chariot, now mended

You healed my foot
It's right that I applaud

Oh gods! Accept my humble foot on a pedestal!

It will look well in your patio
On your drive or by the pool

Think of me fondly
When you gaze on this sculpted foot
Drape towels on it if you wish

Oh, toes of the universe!
Oh, heel and soul don't dishonour me
In the eyes of the gods!

I offer a prayer that none
Suffer bunions, verucas or flaky skin
Gout or impaired balance after wine
May you be honoured by this foot
An enlarged replica of mine

Inspired by a Roman foot sculpture at the British Museum. The owner created it as an offering to the gods after his injured foot was healed.

Michelangelo

'I can see the statue in the marble before I begin work' –
Michelangelo

He sees the statue in the marble

The figure taking form
Yearning to be freed

He feels the muscles flexing
Lungs imbibing air
Hair growing on its scalp

Genitals, calves, proud sternum
Emerging from stone to
The truth of a being

He hears the curl of words
As they escape into a poem

He looks up
Nods in the poet's direction

New Poems

Ulysses in Folkestone

Ulysses came to Folkestone in 1923
500 copies arriving at customs

499 seized for obscenity
What happened to number 500?

Does it lurk somewhere in the old town
Buried in a bookshop
Passed on through generations?

Revered as a bible with its knickers down
Corners turned for the dirty bits
Long superseded by everyday porn

Imagine that curious customs' officer
Passing copy 500 among his friends
Wondering about Dublin, whether
All its girls were as generous as Molly Bloom

The third edition of James Joyce's Ulysses, published by Egoist Press in January 1923, was seized by UK customs at Folkestone.

The Ghost of Franz Kafka

The ghost of Kafka enters the room
Where the poet and his wife are sleeping
He casts a spell and they're forever changed
Married in their dreams on the river Vitava

The boat stops under the Charles Bridge
A flame-haired woman recites vows
She calls on the gods to bless this union
Casts white lilies on the water

Kafka peers at things in the bathroom
He fingers clothes in the closet
Envies the ethnic green shirt
Muses how the purple Chinese dress
Would look good on any woman

He plays with the radio dial
The sleepers hear Mozart in their dreams
Over the many crowned Hradčany
Clouds dispense a chilly Bohemian rain

The writer sneaks down Golden Lane
Plants spells on doors
Plots a formula for turning metal into gold

The sleeping couple stir
Kafka gazes out the window
Anticipating tonight's fireworks
Shower bursting over the forest

The writer examines his reflection
Lean, angular, monochrome
The sleeping couple in the lower half of the frame

New Poems

A cock crows, a pale sun rises in the east
Kafka pads to the door
Joins the maids and early risers in the corridor

Across the city, hangovers alert their owners
To the painful cost of letting go

Kafka slips away, nothing here to see or know

Prague, June

The Ghost of Franz Kafka

More in Sorrow

1

Denied paper, the prisoner adapted
To straitened circumstances, writing with coal
Marking his final days on a prison wall

Resolute, as befits a coming saint
Dipping into principles, set out by faith:

"In faith, I bless you a thousand times," he wrote
"For lending me now some leisure to make rhymes."

2

I first rhymed at a school named Thomas More
We had pens and paper, desks to hide behind
We sinners gave little thought to saints, martyred
Or otherwise, were too busy anticipating the next
Surprise, shuffled from a teenage deck of cards
To spare a prayer for tortured bards

3

Now, to picture a prisoner versifying with coal
Seems profound, to hear the scratch of carbon
On brick, before committing to unyielding ground

More wrote less after losing his head, as poets do when
Newly dead, till comes the resurrection of their reputation
Schools named in honour, now there's completion

Thomas More wrote poetry with pieces of coal while held in the Tower of London in 1535, awaiting death by being hung, drawn and quartered.

New Poems

PART VI - WHERE I AM

The Ghost of Franz Kafka

A Moment With My Map

I take a moment
To work out where I am
What city, which street, whose apartment

The kettle looks familiar
I've seen those slippers before
There are books I'd like to read
But whose coat is hanging on the door?

I trace lines on an imaginary map
Of a country where surrealism is the norm
The guides have taken the night off
The view reveals uncertain forms

I suggest you answer on a postcard
Tell me where I am

September, Brussels

Tigers

We wake at intervals to check
The imminence of sabretooth tigers

The young sleep soundly
Oblivious of danger

They don't know who will disappear
Nor how, nor when

We elders fear night's cloak
Slow hours when tigers prowl

Bite off your leg in a growl
Gobble your brains in a slurp
Suck your guts through gappy gums
Chop chop with hunt-sharp teeth

The young sleep on
We have abandoned innocence
The mountain takes longer to climb
Rear view lost to encroaching mist

A Guardian letter suggested the old wake up frequently because of a primeval instinct to protect the sleeping camp from sabretooth tigers.

The Fools

The Leavers celebrate with Belgian lager
Flick through brochures
For a now more costly Spanish holiday
Plan a day trip to Boulogne
For booze and baccy while they can

The fools were lied to
But they didn't stop to think
Now they take to drink
And mourn their sinking nation
Europe's embarrassing relation

Rule Brittania just an empty slogan
At rainbow's end, no gold, just icy isolation

So wave goodbye to Scotland and to Ireland
Those sensible folk who voted In
Leaving England and Wales to down another gin
No tonic for their sin

The party's over, the hangover begun
Time to bag up all the junk
Common sense has done a bunk
When all is said and done, we're sunk

The Kids Are Alright

Inspired by two children on Radio 4 discussing the EU referendum

What continent are we in?
Are we welcome in France, in Spain?
Or must we settle for British rain
And British food and Britons being rude
To anyone who isn't them

A prospect too grim to contemplate
Teacher says we mustn't hate
Anyone without good reason

But it seems like open season
To challenge strangers in the street
Instead of offering a friendly greet

I don't want to stay when I am grown
You can keep this sad place you call home

Oh, what land, what land is this?
It smells of fish, it's one to miss

Regrets

'On their deathbed, surely no one says they wished they'd gone to more meetings.'
Lisa Pollack, Financial Times, 26 May 2015

On his deathbed
He wished he'd gone to more meetings
Had more delayed train journeys
Waited longer in supermarket queues
Encountered more options when phoning the gas board

Contributed more to work collections
Stayed longer at birthday & Christmas do's
Been more fulsome in praise of idiot managers
Worked on long after retirement age

Forfeiting a globe-trotting pension gap year
An affair with a woman half his age

How much better if there were more dental appointments
More bouts of flu, more spam mail
More sweaty tube journeys
More early morning alarms,
Hurry get dressed there's no time to blink moments

How much better if he wasn't on his deathbed
Heading for God knows where
And he awoke in time to hear someone say
"That covers everything - do you have any questions?"

Yeah Yeah Yeah

Pride of my wardrobe
A cord Beatle jacket with gold buttons

Joy only partly diminished
Because I wasn't *actually* a Beatle
My grey school trousers
No match for my top

There lay the problem
A heart crowded with desires
The reality, a slumbering suburb

Where Mail readers kept their distance
From working class heroes

I was halfway to Heaven
Happy to sign up
When the call came

But the Beatles moved on
Gave up Beatles' jackets
Gave up being Beatles

The dream was over, I woke in an office
Numbed by regulations and routine

The starry world seemed far away
No screaming fans as I boarded the train

Someone, Somewhere in Gold Trainers

She married in Bermuda shorts and gold trainers
After drinking all night with Cuban musicians

Then it was honeymoon time

Two weeks in a van, Europe speeding by
Mountains and lakes cupping the moon

They toured Africa, taught
Reading, writing, bareback-riding

Children came along like buses
Though never three at once

Summer tapped on the door, baubles hung at Christmas
Snow melted beside ambitions

Dreams became muddy as cow pies
The Bermuda shorts hung out to dry

Still there were nights of Cuban music
Golden rum chasing the beat

It was memory time

Someone, somewhere in gold trainers
Turning the corner, pressing a doorbell
Smiling into the surprise of a beautiful new friend

Messages from Paradise

It's a dying art
Encapsulating your experience
In a dozen lines, emphasising the positive
Rejecting the negative, taking care not to boast

The postcard is being replaced by instant messages
Carelessly slapped onto the net

The technicolour landcape
Arriving on the mat exotically stamped
A bright star amongst dingy bills and circulars
Now becoming an endangered species

We should mourn the passing of these snappy snapshots
Messages from paradise that showed you cared

January, Malta

Sawing Wood

I'm sawing wood and humming a poem
While snails gather expectantly
Wondering if sawdust might be tasty as it looks

I'm in the garden sawing wood
Under a clear sky while the elderflower tree
Bends enquiringly toward the noise
And the neighbours' doors stay shut

Keeping the morning to myself
I saw away contentedly
Kerplunk goes another plank
And the secret slow-worm
Wonders if it's safe to emerge

A poet sawing wood is not what he bought into
When he chose this patch of earth
A poet sawing wood, humming a poem to himself

While all the gull-cawing world goes spinning round
And the chalky earth is firm for now
And the almost-silence, almost sound

New Poems

REFERENCE

Patric Cunnane - Biography

The Ghost of Franz Kafka is the ninth collection of poetry from Folkestone-based Patric Cunnane. He also writes short stories and plays.
Patric was born in Purley of Irish parents. His mother, Nora, came from County Clare and his father, Martin, from County Sligo, both situated in the mythical, musical and fabulous west of Ireland.
Along with fellow poet and artist PR Murry, Patric runs Dodo Modern Poets which holds regular events in London and elsewhere. New and established poets present their work to audiences at readings and festivals throughout the UK and Ireland.
In 1984, together with union colleagues, he founded the socialist cabaret, Ragged Trousered Cabaret, to provide entertainment and raise funds for the embattled labour movement during the Thatcher years. RTC can be enjoyed at occasional reunions. Patric was active in performance groups Tongue Circus and Worthless Words in the early eighties.
Other titles by the author include *Dance Music*, *Baltimore* and *Looking For Eden*, published by Dodo Modern Poets and *Roads*, published by Badger Books.
Patric Cunnane is a former Labour councillor in the London Borough of Merton. A journalist by trade, he's had many years experience as NUJ (National Union of Journalists) father of the chapel and chairman of the European Works Council at a large publishing house.

More information on events organised by Dodo Modern Poets: https://dodomodernpoets.wordpress.com.

Palewell Press

Palewell Press is an independent publisher handling poetry, fiction and non-fiction with a focus on human rights, social history and the environment. The Editor may be reached at enquiries@palewellpress.co.uk.

www.ingramcontent.com/pod-product-compliance
Lightning Source LLC
Chambersburg PA
CBHW071032080526
44587CB00015B/2579